What I Wish I Knew
Before I Said "I Do"

The Ultimate Premarital
Relationship Guide for Christians

By Ben Donley

Dedicated to My Other

Table of Contents

Preface

If you want to give yourself the best chance of a forever-love, read this book with your significant other before saying "I Do." Most people who get married do not think hard enough about the specific commitments they are making and, as a result, run into massive relational problems, which threaten to undo their forever-love.

I don't want that to happen to you.

I want you to say, "I will love you forever," and mean it.

Forever!

You don't want to say your "I Do" and then have it become "I Did" and then "I Don't!" This happens a lot – even with you Christian lovers out there. It is better to know what you are getting into with a particular person before diving into a pool that drowns most couples.

I recommend you read this book as a couple and mark it up with your answers and note the questions that pop out of your subsequent conversations with your partner. Then take this book and your notes to a qualified marriage coach, premarital counselor, or pastor and ask them to help you work through what you have discovered.

Warning: This kind of weighty couple introspection might lead you to either postpone your marriage plans until you figure out how to manage your differences or even break off the relationship with the one you are with. But, trust me, it is so much better to back away for a time so you can make wise and informed decisions or permanently end a relationship before the wedding vows are made and you feel 'stuck' with someone you have no business walking through life with.

Okay, so now you have been warned.

Are you ready for a real premarital challenge that will help take you to a genuine forever-love?

If so, read on.

**This relationship book is unlike anything you have ever read in that it tackles topics most other relationship books fail to touch (and does so in fierce but fun ways). Prepare to laugh, squirm, discover, and vastly improve your side of the spousal equation.

Let's begin with a few facts before we launch this book.

Fact #1: Of the two million couples who will get married in the U.S. this year, almost all report they are "more in love than they've ever been" and are "positive about their decision to marry."

Fact #2: Of those two million couples, almost all "expect" to be happily married to their spouse for the rest of their lives. (In other words, not many couples predict an imminent marital decline as they are preparing to say, "I Do.")

Fact #3: Hardly anyone gets married just so they can divorce.

**With these three facts in mind, one must wonder why so many people who boldly proclaim, "I Do," quickly become those who start screaming, "I Do Not."

How does mind-blowing Christian love and marriage transform into iPhone-throwing hate and separation?

Maybe the better question for this relationship book is, "What can you do to make sure these things do not happen to you?"

And the simple answer is this: Do all you can to understand the oft unspoken relational realities facing you and then ask the frequently unanswered questions in this book.

Get some knowledge in the present, and it will prepare you for a bright future. Charge ahead in ignorant bliss, and you will most likely regret it. A passion pursued without knowledge is deadly to marriage (and to most other things in life).

Are you ready to face the realities head-on? If so, let's go…

Reality #1: The Dating Deception

Reality #1: The Dating Deception

Do you really think it's *always* going to 'feel' this good?

Many people are deceived by their chemicals and their 'feels' during the dating, wooing, and falling in love stage of the Forever process. They tend to believe they will feel as good or better about their relationship after marriage as they do during their courtship.

But this is so untrue.

Dating and "falling in love" are marked by massive oxytocin and dopamine rushes. Oxytocin is the "love hormone" that causes warm, fuzzy feelings of total well-being. Dopamine is known as the "pleasure chemical."

Who doesn't want to feel warm and fuzzy all the time?

Who doesn't want pleasure pressed into their heart and mind at a constant clip?

I know I do. But unfortunately, the warm, fuzzy, pleasure releases will come and then go.

Here is some truth to chew on:
Dating/falling in love is the best you are going to 'feel' in a relationship because your happiness chemicals are being cranked to level 11. For some reason, your brain receptors and body pump out happiness and ecstasy at their highest levels when you are falling in love. But this exciting chemical dump does not continue forever. Science says one can expect 6-12 months of this before it fades to normal levels.

But lovers prefer to believe otherwise. Lovers don't follow the science – they follow the 'feels' and believe the 'feels' will go on forever.
(No one says love makes you smart.)

And when you add these temporary fun 'feels' to the following dating/mating rituals, you have an almost guaranteed "I Do" in the making.

What are the Dating Rituals?

How do these Dating Rituals encourage an *un*-informed decision to commit to an "I Do?"

I suggest you turn the page and find out...

Dating Ritual #1: Argument Avoidance makes us feel like we have found our true soul mate. Agreements about pretty much everything make everything seem rosy.

"I'll be your Yes, Yes, Yes-Man/Woman even when something deep down screams, "No, No, No!"

Who doesn't love it when someone agrees with them? Who doesn't *really* love it when someone they love agrees with them? "So baby, let's be agreeable and keep these fun chemicals going. Let's do argument avoidance. We can whip out the disagreements during the honeymoon…."

Dating Ritual #2: Attraction to someone *and* being attractive to that same someone gives a jump to the emotional battery.

"I want you to want me, and you want me to want you, so let's just do that. Being wanted is intoxicating. So, let's stay drunk on that."

We all try hard to be attractive. We want others to see us and think, "That there is a good-looking, good-smelling, good-thinking, good-sense of humoring, good-catch for my life. I want to reel that fish in." And when that fish bites the bait, our hearts leap. You know how it goes – any time you catch someone staring at you with longing, it's an excitement explosion. And when this look progresses to a date and then to a dating relationship, you will be feeling quite extraordinary. Just seeing your person makes your heart go pitter-patter, and knowing that you make their heart go pitter-patter is super fun. And when this leads to physical compliments – "you look beautiful" – "you are as hot as the sun" – our chemical pops go to another level, and our insecurities get assassinated. It feels fantastic to want someone who wants you, to hear that you are attractive, and to bypass insecurity for a while. And this fantastic feeling typically turns off the thinking switch we need to make intelligent relational decisions.

Dating Ritual #3: Approvals that make us pop.

Just as much as we love agreement, we thirst for approval, and dating gives us gallons of it. Drink up, daters!

Relational rejection sucks. Nobody is going to disagree with that unless they are an emotional sadist. But relational approval rocks the world because it tells you are acceptable and accepted for all you are and all you do. Most of us live to be approved and accepted. So, cue the dating relationship: LOLs and smiles and heart emojis shot at your clever jokes plus nodding, deep-thought furrowed brows at your intellectual takes on everything are chemical pushers that push aside the thinker inside of us who wants us to think before we "I Do."

19

Dating Ritual #4: Applause and encouragement from an audience you care about.

"2-4-6-8. Who do I appreciate? You, you, you!!!"

Cheerleading about who you are, who you want to become, and what you have already done goes a long way to keeping the love claws in deep. Cheerleaders are encouragers who can pep you up no matter what.

When you feel self-doubt, but you have a cheerleader, you have someone there to lift you up and out. "Hang in there" and "I know you can do it" makes a person feel bolder. Being encouraged about your dreams to become a Space-X astronaut who will win the Nobel Prize someday really makes you feel good, especially when your dumb parents think you should stick to plumbing or accounting. In dating, it's all pom-poms and cheers, and both of those can distract you and drown out what your logic might be trying to say.

Dating Ritual #5: Being someone else's focus and priority

"You are my #1 and the spicy chili on my front burner."

Knowing that someone else would drop anything to take care of you and be with you is empowering.

Dating Ritual #6: Physicality and the touchy-touchy, kissy-kissy

Making out is a buzz-fest! Hands intertwined, Burt's Bees lips on Carmex lips, bodies pressed together, etc., is dizzying.

Electric shock waves and sexual energy pulsing with anything from a handhold to a repentance-inducing clothes-tearing-off scenario is hard to beat. "Hooking-up" (whatever that means for you) blinds the best of us from seeing as clearly as we ought.

Dating Ritual #7: Résumé pushing

"Yes, I am here to apply for the position of president of your corporation. I have no weaknesses, only strengths."

We tend to share our best accomplishments and attributes in this 'love interview' because we want the other person to hire us forever. We dare not share our failures or brokenness and risk ending the good feelings we feel. And when we see the other person's spotless résumé without any troubling life typos, we believe it without a background check and make them our #1 candidate.

Dating Ritual #8: Thoughtful gifts

"Awww. A mini-llama. Thanks, boyfriend. I've always wanted one."

Through enhanced 'interested listening' techniques, we gather up bits of information about what things this person would love to have in their possession. Then we give these gifts and receive these gifts, and this special gift-giving makes us pop with happiness.

So those are the most common and successful "Dating Rituals," and boy, oh boy, do they ever push couples to keep rolling forward. They are definitely catalysts for long-term commitments.

Why?

All the above Dating Rituals will ding your dopamine doorbells and activate your oxytocin pumps to never before felt levels. They will also hook your emotions, making you feel "high" on life and love.

So, to review, we have chemicals cranking, emotions hooked, and abounding positivity full-blasting between you and your significant other. That's a lot and usually enough to get you both to commit to an "I Do."

But wait, there's more...
More dinging, activating, and popping marriage catalysts that will float in and convince you that you are on the right track in your relationship.

Check out these Love Poppers and consider how they could be adversaries to logical

decision-making.

Love Popper #1: Cultural Excitement

Culture loves to tell us to find and get married to our "soul mate." So, when you are in a serious dating relationship, it feels like the entire world is behind you with a proud hand on your shoulder. "This is what you are meant for, and we, the universe, are for you!"

Love Popper #2: Friends and Family Excitement

We all have friends and family who get giddy about our relational successes. They ask probing questions and congratulate us on discovering relational gold. Their excitement drives our excitement. Their approvals and applause just give us that much more dopamine and adrenaline.

Love Popper #3: Anticipations of what surprises are coming next

Life is boring most of the time. We usually don't have much fun to anticipate. But falling in love and heading into marriage lets you shake off the normal boredom for a time and gives you plenty of fun things to anticipate.

The proposal is coming! How will it go?
The showers are coming! Who will be there to shower me?
The gifts are coming! What beautiful, cool stuff will we be able to get others to buy for us?
The ceremony is coming! How magical will this prince and princess celebration be?
The honeymoon is coming! Will we do Europe or Hawaii?
Sexual freedom is coming! How good will it feel to be completely physically intimate without shame or guilt?

There are a lot of fun things to anticipate, right? And they all come with the 'falling in love' package.

Okay – now review all the above and tell me how great it all seems – how great it all is. The combination of happiness hormones, dopamine drives, emotional hooks, cultural acceptance, support from those you trust, intimacy, etc., would make anyone feel almost perfect about their relationship.

And when something feels this great, what do most of us tend to do?

Simple - We do whatever we can to keep these feelings going. We become addicts to these rare-air chemicals, dating rituals, and boredom killers because they feel so amazing. And like an addict, we say, "Let's keep the party rolling and stay high."

Here's the downer: The addiction to this feels-based "love" will not lead to a love that lasts. This 'feelings' version of "love" fades.

Science says so. Experience says so. Stats say so. Married couples say so. But because most of us enjoy the feelings brought on by the whole dating package, we tend to push away/disregard clear thinking that might disrupt the pleasure dumps.

Who cares about reality and truth and knowledge-gathering when swimming in oceans of ignorant, chemical, and cultural bliss?

Here's the point I am trying to make:
It's nice to feel good! But you ***need*** to counter the 'feels' with clear thinking about what is to

come when all the realities hit you smack in the face – and they will. They hit everyone. Some are ready for the realities; most are not.

I'm here to get you ready.

Here is some truth to consider: When you are seriously dating, it's like a visit to the Louvre where you can't take your eyes off the striking, never before seen or experienced, Mona Lisa. But when you get married, it's like getting a janitorial job at that same Louvre. You see the same Mona Lisa over and over, day after day, and that changes things. That which was uncommon and special at the start becomes common and less special. Your Mona Lisa becomes just another painting on the wall, and you start wondering whether the price tag of 'forever' is worth it.

While you are dating, you need to ask yourself the following questions:

-What happens when the love chemicals stop pumping?

-What happens when you don't 'feel' like you did in the wooing and winning process?

-What happens when the agreements turn into disagreements?

-What happens when the smiles turn into frowns?

-What happens when your cheerleader begins booing your missed lay-ups?

-What happens when your significant

other's perfections are overwritten by significant imperfections?

-What happens when you (or they) unpack all the wounds, brokenness, odd ideas, weird thoughts, and idiosyncrasies from their real-life suitcase, and you see that what you now have is not what you thought you said "yes" to?

-What happens when culture, family, and friends stop applauding?

What happens when all the anticipations have passed and standard boredom kicks in every day?

Let me tell you what happens with even the most promising Christian couples.
We will call this Reality #2...

Reality #2: The Mindset Changes

Reality #2: The Mindset Changes

When we are dating a person who we think is extra-special, we usually have a Winner's mindset. We see someone with whom we want to be connected, and we do all we can to win their heart.

So, to do this, we go out of our way to prove that we, above any other challengers, are the top choice for their relational satisfaction.

We speak all five love languages fluently, keep our breath minty fresh, and bathe our bodies regularly (possibly even using a loofah and expensive, pheromone-boosting soaps). We discover fashion that is pleasing to our target's eye, etc.

But when most people step out of the wedding ceremony, hand in hand with their gold medal spouse, things change.

At this moment of victory, we think we have already won and no longer feel the need to be in winner mode. And thus, we tend to change our mindset from **Winner to Owner**.

"I have you, and you have me."

And once this shift happens in our heads, a terrible shift happens in our actions.

What occurs?

As Owners, we relax. We stop doing what we did when we were in Winner mode. We quit doing what we did to win that person's heart. We function like, "This person is mine now. I cannot lose them." And then the worst thing of all happens: We begin to take our spouses for granted.

And when we take our spouses for granted, we start to lose them. We move from Heart-Winners to Heart-Losers.

It happens all the time.

(Now, I know this next section is jumping ahead of the dating game and onto married life, but I bring it up here simply to prep you for it now and get you thinking about how you might avoid losing your Love in the future…)

Acting like Losers:
What does "losing" look like?
-Moving from Multi-lingual to Mute
When we are winning, we speak every love language in the book. We give gifts. We offer our most quality time. We serve them. We

speak uplifting and encouraging words. We comfort and even make them feel cared for with our physical touch.

But post-ceremony, after we no longer have that *healthy pressure* to do so, we pull back. We go mute. We slow down on the gifts, take back our time, groan at having to serve, use our words for "house business," and slow down/stop the affectionate touching.

-The Priority List Shifts

When we are winning, our significant other is placed at the very top of our list, and everything else is ordered below them. This person receives all our attention because they are our most important pursuit. But after we successfully 'capture' them, our "significant other" gets much less significant as they are taken out of the front seat and off the front burner. They get moved back.

Moved back to where?

Moved back down below *everything* that was ranked high on the "life list" before that person entered the picture. *Everything* - including endless career ladders, childhood friendships, unfulfilled dreams, unseen movies, unseen television series, unfinished video games, unPinned recipes, shopping lists, other people, cool events, unvisited vacation spots, and other *un-owned* opportunities.

Those take precedence. Most of the time, it is a subconscious re-prioritizing because nobody really writes "tossing the love of my life to the back burner" on a literal to-do list. Still, the reality happens and can be seen in the behavior of one or both marriage participants.

-The Anti-Love happens

Somehow when we are dating, we are able to accomplish the best version of "love" more than ever. As Winners, we tend to be patient, kind, trusting, humble, truthful, forgiving, and selfless.

But as Owners, we not only stop loving like this, but we also begin to distribute what I call "the Anti-Love." We treat our spouses with selfishness, impatience, unkindness, jealousy, competitiveness, a lack of forgiveness, and pride.

-Baggage Claim Time

When we are winning our partners' hearts, we do not usually parade around our unstable emotional, mental, and spiritual baggage. In Winner mode, we understand that carrying this sort of crazy life baggage around is scary to potential suitors. If we want people to take lifetime trips with us, we know that we had better not show up to the "Marriage Airport" with more than a small suitcase and a carry-on. Yes, we may reveal some of our more minor issues, but nothing that will alarm the ones we love.

But, when we do *land* our partners and the marriage happens, most of us believe it will be okay if we go ahead, grab all our semi-psycho luggage off the airport carousel (that we so carefully checked before take-off), and then ask our partners to help us carry it.

This can be a shocking event when the Owner of said baggage gets past the Honeymoon and then must rent three Smart Carts to load on massive trunks packed tight with past rejections, insecurities, anger, bitterness, family addiction patterns, and unhealed wounds.

These get rolled to the car and then carried into the marriage.

Eyes get wide when this sort of unpacking begins.

"Can all that crap really be yours, sweetheart?"
Sweetheart nods his/her head, but not sweetly.

-We stop trying to be attractive

When we are trying to woo our spouses, we do all we can to put on our best faces. But as Owners, we put our best faces away and often stop trying to be attractive at all. We think that it is unnecessary to attract our mates once we get married. We act as if their life commitments to us give us a license to *let ourselves go.*

Our Ugly Reality becomes 3-D.
Our morning breath goes unchecked. The bathroom door is left open during what used to be private stench sessions. Toilets go unwiped. Anti-stink **Febreze** goes unsprayed. Body odor is allowed to reign. Diets are abandoned,

42

workouts are skipped, pounds are added, lips are left chapped, and we let ourselves go on one-way trips to unattractiveness. We get gross, act impolitely, and assume that our partners' sensory organs are dead.

-Role changes

When we are actively winning people's hearts, we smartly take on the role of lover and ally. These are the parts we play. These roles define the script we speak. They guide the actions we take. But when we become Owners, we often exchange our positive roles for negative ones. Instead of lifting our partners up, we become critics who give thumbs down to most of their moves. Instead of applauding their goodness, we become nags who demand quick changes. Instead of acting as their equal partners in the business of marriage, we take on the role of boss and act as if they owe us quality work.

No Surprise: Nobody enjoys a micromanaging critic trying to mold them into a desired shape. This will not work for long.

Now I am not saying that everyone reading this book will go from being a Heart Winner to becoming a full-scale Heart Loser. But almost without exception, marriage participants display some of the behavioral shifts described above.

And if you intentionally or unintentionally go in this direction with your future mindset and your actions, I have something very important to write to you here: You may "have" your partner legally, but by 'owning' them, you will lose them daily. And you will deserve to lose them. The love you are earning and the heart you are winning now will be lost.

Here is the simple summary equation you

should memorize now: Winners who become Owners become Losers. This is not to say that you will necessarily lose your marriage and end up alone, but I can pretty much guarantee that the love your partner had for you before the "I Do" will wane.

And since marriage is supposed to be a relationship filled with love, a marriage that begins leaking love will feel flat very soon.

Unfortunately, like the chemical and hormonal explosions mentioned in Reality #1, the good, pre-marriage behaviors are often short-lived. Heart-winners usually become heart-owners, and with that subsequent mindset shift, words and behaviors shift to the less happy and fun.

So, knowing this is common, consider these questions in your present:

45

*What do you need to do to make sure you don't shift from heart-winner to heart-owner to heart-loser?

*How can you stop yourself from taking your lover for granted? From putting them on the back burner?

*What will you do if you sense that your partner is making this negative shift? What will you do if you notice this shift in yourself?

One of the leading causes of divorce and cheating, even for good Christians, is that one or both people within the marriage stop(s) doing what they did before they got married.

Recommendation: Don't. Instead, commit to continue doing whatever you are doing in dating mode after the dating blooms into marriage.

Reality #3: Time spent together after you get married will look very different than it does now.

Reality #3: Time spent together after you get married will look very different than it does now.

At the beginning of a relationship, people tend to save their best time for their best person. But once married, this tends to shift.

Let's consider a 'normal' day for two working partners: Both partners wake up tired, rush around trying to get prepped for workdays at different locations, mostly thinking about what stuff they must get done once there. Most morning conversations between couples are about the stresses to come or about how one needs to stop stealing the sink and mirror space. Talk tends to be snippy, snappy, and short. Then both spouses go on to their respective workplaces and give their best energies and efforts to tasks that tax them. Work is tiring. They also must give their emotional energies to bosses, colleagues, and clients.

When both partners get home around 6 o'clock, they are typically wiped out. They have given their best and their most-est to live up to their employment résumés so as not to get fired and maybe even to get a promotion – definitely to get a paycheck. With all this effort and energy expended, there isn't a whole lot more to give upon arrival at the home base. Both partners are exhausted and would prefer to be served and pampered. Both partners usually want to download their days to one another – to talk about the successes and failures and maybe do a bit of complaining. But sometimes, one or both partners prefer(s) just to be quiet, unwind, de-stress, and be left alone. Either way, it's not fun, quality-time enjoyed like it was back in the dating days.

Following this initial re-connection, partners face things to be done: food to be prepped or ordered, household chores to be done, and if there are kids, well, that's an entirely different level of busyness to deal with. When all that is dealt with, most of the rest of the night is spent in front of the TV until bedtime. Sex and/or romantic gestures might happen, but usually, one or both 'lovers' are too tired to indulge or initiate that kind of loving.

Then they both sleep and wake up and do it all over again. Weekends can be good times to re-connect with your partner, but often become hours used to hang with family, catch up on stuff that didn't get done during the week, and prep for the looming work week. And if you do have children, weekends (not to mention weeknights) are spent running them around to soccer games, ballet recitals, and friends' birthday parties.

51

I am not guaranteeing this will be *your* time-spent cycle, but it is for most couples I have coached. After marriage, time spent together is usually not as fun as it once was. It's important to know this so you can lower your expectations, be more intentional in carving out better time for your spouse and offer grace to the other tired human in your house.

An author's note: Scheduling weekly date nights to counter this is not as effective as you might think. Date nights, if they actually happen, will not be the salvation for your love relationship. Sometimes it is better to just accept the reality of how times have changed and adjust accordingly.

Here are some good questions for you to consider before you get married regarding how time will be spent:

52

*How will you prepare your schedules so the time you spend together is still quality time?

*What strategies can you put into place now, so you don't give the best of yourself at work and with other relationships?

*How can you make sure you reserve some of your best self for the spouse whom you will see after long days?

Reality #4: Your Deep Beliefs matter a whole lot more than you think.

Reality #4: Your Deep Beliefs matter a whole lot more than you think.

Many Christian people I have coached assume that they are golden if they find a cool person who claims they are Christian. But the truth is, you need to make the effort and take the time to drill down and dig into what you and the other person truly believe about the Bible and God. And then, you need to move beyond theology and doctrine and find out how much these spiritual beliefs translate into practice.

Why is this so important?

There are many versions of Christian belief and Christian practice these days. The word 'Christian' doesn't mean the same thing to everyone. And if your version of Christianity and the practice of it doesn't match your partner's version, it can lead to destruction.

Your task: Ask and answer the following questions to determine how closely your versions of Christianity match up.

The Deepest Questions

*Do you believe the entire Bible is the inspired Word of God?

*How well do you know the Bible? How many times have you read all of it? How important do you think it is to read and study the Bible?

*What is the point of the Bible's message?

*Is God good? What does this even mean?

*Do you agree that submitting to Jesus' Lordship is crucial to being saved? In other words, do you believe that what God says about right and wrong is unquestionable, and are you surrendered to His code regardless of what culture says?

*Is your theology based on what the whole Bible teaches, or is it based on some human's version of what it says? In other words, would you say you align yourself with a traditional theology/theologian, or do you form your own theology based on your reading of the Bible as a whole?

*What do you believe about the Holy Spirit and the gifts He gives to God's people?

*What do you think about "Progressive Christianity?" "Deconstruction?"

*What is your prayer life like? What do you think prayer is for?

57

*Do you have an intimate relationship with God in which His love for you is experiential (a love that surpasses knowledge)? How do you foster that sort of intimacy? Do you believe you can access God's presence and relate to Him yourself, or do you look for others to be your go-between?

*What do you believe the point of your life is? Why do you think you were created?

*What equals success to you? How important is money, position, stuff, and other people's approval?

*Do you see yourself as an alien and a stranger on this Earth, or are you heavily involved in capturing all that *the world* offers?

*Do you love *the world* or anything in it?
Or do you reject *the world system* as a 'trash
substitute' for the Kingdom of God that is
coming? (I John 2:15-17)

*What do you think about the Lord's
Prayer? God's Will?

*How important do you think it is to be an
involved servant within a local church? Do
you know what spiritual gifts you have been
given?

*What is your take on tithing? How
important do you think this is?

*How important is it to you to become a
true disciple of Jesus Christ? What do you

think this means?

*How does your Christianity inform your politics? Is your own political platform one that matches your Christian beliefs? Pro-Life? Pro-God's design? Do you believe more in the Constitution or the Bible?

*Does your Christianity shape the way you take in media so you are able to un-spin it, or does media shape the way you see the world? How important is social media to you, and why?

*How does your Christianity impact your decision-making? Do you seek God before making decisions and wait on Him, or do you just decide on stuff and hope God covers it?

*How does grace affect your self-perception? What would you say is your determined and unshakeable identity?

*How does Christianity affect how you relate to people?

*Do you seek approval from people and the world more than you seek God's approval? Are you more of a people-pleaser or a God-pleaser?

*Do you have anyone to keep you accountable in your life?

*What sin patterns do you have? What sin secrets do you carry? What are you most tempted by?

*What Christian beliefs and practices are you looking for in a marriage partner?

*What beliefs and practices *must* be present in your significant other for you to commit to them forever?

*Are you actively pursuing/pushing for a more 'just' world?

*Do you believe that prayer has the power to demolish strongholds, arguments, and pretensions that set themselves against the knowledge of God? Do you pray with this power to shake up this messed-up world?

*Do you think you have a "no matter what happens" sort of faith in God, or is your faith dependent on good circumstances and outcomes? What potential adverse events or situations might lead you to question your faith or walk away from God? Ever been disappointed by God?

*What doubts or questions do you have about faith in God? In the Bible? In Christianity?

*What is your church background? Church preference? Worship background? Worship preference? How important is it that you are in a church that meets your needs/wants?

*How seriously do you take spiritual warfare? Do you believe you are surrounded by enemy powers and principalities who hope to devour you? Do you believe in a literal Heaven and Hell?

*Do you believe it is essential to be involved in evangelism? How do you engage in it?

Now I know that was a lot to tackle, but this is such a huge deal. If you don't know what you really believe and/or what your potential life partner really believes about spiritual matters, it could be the worst thing for your relationship. A successful Christian marriage relationship depends on shared beliefs and practices with God at the center. And if you go into marriage assuming your version of Christianity is the same as your partner's version, but it turns out to be quite different, you are in for some significant battles the enemy will use to break you down and break you up.

Here are three examples of Christian assumption gone bad:

*Angela, a lifetime Lutheran, marries Michael who is the non-denominational sort. Angela assumes Michael has similar beliefs and practices until one Sunday dinner at Angela's parents' house, Michael is asked to pray for the meal of roast and potatoes. Michael nods, smiles, raises his arms above his head, launches into a long, fiery prayer and then starts speaking in tongues before closing with a powerful "Amen!" Angela's mother passes out at the table as her father stares at Michael wide-eyed wondering if his son-in-law is possessed or just fluent in both Ugaritic and Spanish. The roast and potatoes are blessed, but they *are* a bit cold.

*Mandy and Richard are happily married Christians who never really talked about their versions of Christianity before they said, "I Do!" And on most spiritual issues it turns out, they agree. But when they are setting up their first budget, Mandy writes up a line item for Tithe, expecting her beloved to be excited about giving a baseline 10% of their gross income to the church they attend. But her beloved is not excited. In fact, he takes out a sharpie and draws a thick black line through that line item insisting there is no way they are going to give even 1% to their church.

*Fiona, a Four-Square Fundamentalist, assumes that her handsome beau, Fred, believes the same about the Bible as she does. But during their newlywed Bible study at her home church, Fred laughs out loud when the leader says that God created everything in a literal seven days. "I don't think so, bro," he says while lovingly squeezing Fiona's hand. Then he tosses in this classic, "I hope you don't also think Jonah was swallowed by a fish. I believe in God, but c'mon, science and logic trump these myths." He looks at an enraged Fiona, who has angrily dropped his hand and says, "Right, babe?"

Three examples that remind us: It might be a good idea to ask some spiritual questions before the marriage. It might be a good idea to clarify the details of your version of Christian belief and practice before you run into a soul-surprise.

Now my wife and I do not have the exact same spiritual beliefs, practices, preferences, or giftings. But we had a very good idea as to each other's versions of Christianity before heading into our marriage.

No assumptions = No surprises. Thank God.

On soul issues, we matched up and we still match up. We both believe in the fundamentals, seek intimacy with God as priority, allow the Bible to be our final word for settling disputes, accept Jesus's Lordship instead of demanding our own selfish rights, let grace and faith be our guide in this jacked-up system, and we see the world with the same perspective. As a result, we have a fun, relaxed, and stress-free relationship. Neither of us ever worries that the other is going to jump to the dark side, which is nice because there are plenty of other difficult and unpredictable parts of marriage to deal with.

I hope you take this recommendation seriously: Do not assume on the deeper things unless you enjoy unpleasant surprise parties.

Reality #5: Life storms will hit you and your significant other.

Reality #5: Life storms will hit you and your significant other.

Bad stuff happens in life. Hard junk happens to everyone. Storms come. Tragic circumstances, wicked people, crushed expectations, dream death, tragic loss, unfair decisions, unexpected rejections, disease diagnoses, etc., will smack into you, no matter how well you try to protect yourself.

And when these experiences enter the picture, they can change you and/or the person you love. These hardships can cause depression, brokenness, anxiety, fear, stress, and limitation, which can turn you and/or your spouse into different creatures.

Let me drive this home with some **"Not Fun with Dick and Jane"** examples you should

71

examine as if they were happening to you.

1. Dick loses his job and cannot find employment for more than a year. Jane works full-time, but they still cannot afford to pay their bills. Dick feels worthless, rejected, and experiences a real loss of identity. After trying for hundreds of jobs and not being hired, Dick feels like giving up. Jane comes home from work every day tired and stressed about their rising credit card debt while feeling extremely sad for her husband. But she also feels frustrated at him because he doesn't even shower in the morning and spends most of his day playing video games while drinking beer they certainly cannot afford.

2. Dick and Jane have a lovely young girl named Stephanie, whom they work hard

to raise right. Because they both work full-time, Dick and Jane leave Stephanie with a trusted caregiver. But one day, a terrible accident occurs, and Stephanie is killed. No one is at fault, but Dick and Jane are still left with the reality of the tragedy of loss. Jane wants to go to a pastoral counselor, but Dick, who used to be the strong spiritual leader of the home, is so angry at God that he refuses to go. In his anger and sadness, Dick chooses to start living on barstools and drowning his depression in alcohol. As months go forward, Dick and Jane grow apart. They both despise the others' choices for 'healing,' and when they are together, all they do is argue.

3. Dick and Jane are living the American Dream – 3 adorable kids, a lovely home,

excellent salaries, a solid Bible study
community, etc. One day at a routine
checkup, Dick finds out he has stage 4
cancer and has about 6 months to live.
The entire family is floored by this news,
and their Christian community is as well.
And despite tons of love and support
coming to them from every side, Dick
starts to question his faith. He meets an
old friend who introduces him to
deconstruction and Dick decides to
make edits to his belief system. As
Dick's health grows worse, his unbelief
grows stronger. He tells Jane that he no
longer believes in a God who would give
him cancer.

4. Dick and Jane are lower-middle-class but
   happy and in love. They have a kind-
   hearted 10-year-old boy named Jimmy,

for whom they would do anything. Things are not easy on the financial front, but they always set money aside for Jimmy to go to Church Summer Camp with his friends. He is always enriched by it, and Dick and Jane see it as a must for him. But at Summer Camp this year, Jimmy is sexually molested by a counselor and returns home a different kid. He is consumed with shame and feels like filth, but he doesn't tell anyone about it. He starts hanging out with some guys who introduce him to drugs that make Jimmy feel the numbness he craves.

I could go on and on with Dick and Jane's 'reality' stories, but I think you get the point, and I am sure Dick and Jane would prefer I don't drop any more storms on them.

But these kinds of stories happen all the time to people like you and me. And if we do not ready ourselves for the storms that Jesus guarantees, we will get shaken and often toss away our marriages and our faith as the troubles hit.

The absolute best marriages get destroyed by such things. Just being honest…

Let me say a bit more about this because it is such a huge deal. In many marriages, the following vow is said: "I will love you for better or for worse."

Here is the follow-up question to that vow: What about when "worse" happens?

"For better or for worse…."

'Better' is great. We all want that. If we were handed a life menu by a genie waiter who asks us to order whatever we want, most of us will order a huge plate of 'better' every day. Who doesn't love it when life improves? Who doesn't love it when they get a promotion, a raise, cool gifts, deeper connections with their partner, cute children, a lottery win, or a royal flush?

It is easy to feel good when our circumstances and situations leap up near where we want them to be. Desires are being met, and everything seems to be blue sky. Our responses to 'better' usually lead to celebrations and smiles and thanksgivings. With 'better', we proclaim contentment.

But circumstances and situations tend to fluctuate in all areas of life, and unfortunately, they fluctuate into the depths for extended periods.

77

What I Wish I Knew Before I Said "I Do" | Ben Donley

In other words, life craters. And when life craters and tough circumstances cut across the Achilles heel of our 'better' desires, we often respond with anger, confusion, frustration, attacks, and complaint.

And these responses, when they extend and expand for a long time, are not good for marriages. When one or both spouses in a marriage are fighting for their lives and grabbing for some of that old 'better,' trying to regain what had been normal but now seems like a grand dream, the relationship is given less focus. If hopes are deferred or unfulfilled, there is much gnashing of teeth and very little love shared.

Two people holed up in a cave of 'worse' is like double darkness. And if it is just one partner undergoing the 'worse,' it can be even more challenging to deal with.

Why?

There is supposed pressure on the person living out the 'better' to help the one undergoing struggle, which is not easy.

Another dangerous part of the 'worse' is that it tends to lead to either singular or coupled escapism. In other words, one or both persons in the marriage try to find adequate worldly comforters, which can temporarily pull them out of the drowning pool. Because the desperation and despair of the 'worse' crowds out rational decision-making, a spouse you think would never do anything stupid can really hurt your partnership by diving into different sorts of feel-good escapes and/or feel-good people who are willing to give them what they think they need.

Most people are not good storm survivors. Not

many of us drive well in the icy rain and hail. Our cars tend to slide all over the road, scaring the crap out of our spouses who happen to be passengers on these unforeseen rides.

So, I want to just say to all of you married and soon-to-be-married humans out there:

There is *better*. There is *worse*. And there is even *worst*.

That's the reality.

You need to figure out how to help each other celebrate the former without depending on it and to get through the latter two without letting them get between you.

Consider the following questions regarding this reality:

*What if a worst-case scenario happens to

you? To your spouse? To both of you?

*What are your imagined worst-case scenarios:

- Financially?
- Relationally?
- Vocationally?
- Physically / Health-wise?
- Emotionally?
- Spiritually?

*How do you typically respond to situations when they get worse?

*What do you think are the best ways to deal with difficult life changes?

*How will you prepare for the harsh realities this world and our spiritual enemies have in store for you?

Reality #6: Both you and your significant other will become less and less physically attractive.

Reality #6: Both you and your significant other will become less and less physically attractive.

If you are getting married to someone primarily because they are pretty or handsome, you are in for problems as time goes on. I know this might shock you, but as people get older, they get less physically attractive.

And no matter how much Botox is injected or plastic surgery is performed, your partner will never be the same kind of sexy as before the age-erosion.

Are you ready to be married to a wrinkled, balding human with an ever-growing nose and ever-extending ears?

Are you cool with being married to a fatter, softer version of who you said "I Do" to?

Can you love the physically unattractive person who will slowly appear before your eyes?

Can you love them as you once did, especially if you hold onto your looks longer than they do?

Can you love them even when someone younger and more attractive comes along and expresses interest in you? (Because this will probably happen…)

Will you toss your old, unattractive mate aside, or will your love go beyond the skin-deep sort?

If you are marrying someone mainly because they look good, expect a short marriage. Just saying…

"When You Are Old" by William Butler Yeats

When you are old and grey and full of sleep,
And nodding by the fire, take down this book,
And slowly read, and dream of the soft look
Your eyes had once, and of their shadows deep;

How many loved your moments of glad grace,
And loved your beauty with love false or true,
But one man loved the pilgrim soul in you,
And loved the sorrows of your changing face;

And bending down beside the glowing bars,
Murmur, a little sadly, how Love fled
And paced upon the mountains overhead
And hid his face amid a crowd of stars.

"When I'm 64" by The Beatles

When I get older losing my hair
Many years from now
Will you still be sending me a Valentine
Birthday greetings bottle of wine...
Will you still need me, will you still feed me
When I'm sixty-four (74? 84? 94?)

85

Reality #7: Affinities do matter.

Reality #7: Affinities do matter.

The first truth is: Opposites do attract.

The second and more important truth is: Attracted Opposites rarely have good marriages for long.

Third and most important truth: It's better to find someone more like you than someone significantly different from you.

This is where I make my case for how shared affinities matter a lot.

The music you like, the hobbies you enjoy, the movies and TV shows you prefer will matter because we spend a lot of our shared free time on these things. If you love listening to Radiohead and your partner cherishes listening to the soundtrack of **Cocomelon**, road trips are going to be tough. If you love Hallmark movies and they love violent, foreign series on Netflix, your remote control will become a weapon of war. Suppose they love **The Godfather,** and you think it's overrated, especially compared with the genius of **Air Bud** or Marvel flicks. In that case, I'll bet there might be some serious judgment and even disgust that arises between you. If your idea of a fun vacation is all-things Vegas and your partner thinks Vegas is for morons and instead wants to book a mud spa retreat in the Himalayas, I am guessing you will vacation separately. If for them a fun weekend means deep cleaning the baseboards and gardening, while for you a great weekend means golfing with your buddies, I doubt there will be much marital peace on Saturdays and Sundays – your marriage will be under par. And under par marriages are not as fun as under par golf.

This might all sound ridiculous and small to you. But take my word for it, affinities matter. What entertains you, entertains you for a reason. And if you get married to someone who has polar-opposite entertainments, it is going to be a painful coupling – especially if either of you offers your negative opinions (judgments) about what the other one enjoys. It might be a good idea to discuss your affinities with your potential mate *now*. You can only fake liking their Garth Brooks mixes for so long…

The Flip-Side: That being said, just because two people really, really like the same music, the same movies, the same television shows, the same style of hipster eyewear, the same restaurants, the same type of beer, and the same political party, does not mean they should get married.

Yes, it is true that compatibility and shared affinities typically link people into fun friendships. And yes, it is nice when these things exist within a marriage.

But, as many "compatible" couples find out after moving from the fun, romantic dating relationship into a busy and often stressful marriage relationship, a life together is not built solely on what you both enjoy. Unfortunately, couples do not often realize this truth until they've already locked in for life. Many couples are easily fooled by the compatibility motivation because there is the thought that, "I've finally found someone who is a lot like me because they like what I like. We have too much in common for this not to be a workable lifelong

90

partnership." This is a mistake for many reasons: the compatibility focus is on external similarities, which usually change over time. As well, people often temporarily *like what you like* because they want to be in a relationship with you and don't want anything to get in the way of perfection.

In conclusion, if you can find a person with whom you are highly compatible and who also passes some deeper, internal tests for a lifetime partnership, you are a blessed human being. But do not let yourself fall in love with someone you would do better going to Coachella with once a year.

Reality #8: There are some basic qualifications for marriage.

Reality #8: There are some basic qualifications for marriage.

What makes you think you are qualified for marriage?

Before you try to confidently answer in the affirmative, let's begin with an even more fundamental question: Is there a minimal skill set required to succeed at marriage?

Quick answer: YES!!!

If working at McDonald's requires a minimal skill set and some basic pre-floor training so that customers don't die, then marriage most definitely has a set of suggested skills, which makes a partner less likely to fail in their "Super-Sized, Extra-Value" marriage.

In fact, the skill set I believe is required for marriage is so vast and multi-faceted, I am amazed that anyone even attempts lifetime coupling without first proving themselves worthy by training with both Navy Seals and Great White Sharks.

I am pretty sure that the "necessary" skill set for a successful marriage requires that sort of high-level Special Forces toughness to go along with verbal and non-verbal communication expertise, high-level emotional intelligence, otherworldly spiritual connections, mind-reading abilities, a Gandhi-like humility, and the flexibility of a Cirque de Soleil performer.

Do many people have this high-level skill set crucial to operating a successful marriage?

Quick answer: NO!!!
Do *you* have the skills?

Well, let's see if you do —

Answer the following questions to see if you have all the skills or if you need some serious on-the-job training as I did. (As you answer these questions, realize that no one is perfect and that no one completely qualifies at the beginning. But if you allow this little quiz to bring you some awareness of the skills you need and add this awareness to a commitment to learn, change, and grow, you will have a much better chance of becoming a high-functioning and qualified spouse.)

Marriage Qualification Quiz

• **Do you give up easily?** If you give up easily, you lack a crucial skill needed for a successful marriage.

- **How have you ever persevered through difficulty?** If you aren't the persevering type, you are missing an essential skill.

- **What do you think about "double lives?" Do you hide things about yourself from people?** If you are like Dr. Jekyll and Mr. Hyde and are a secret keeper, you are not a keeper. You are missing the skill of truthful transparency.

- **Are you a patient listener?** If you don't know how to give full attention to someone while they are talking about life with you, you aren't skilled enough for marriage. If you **must** check your text messages while someone else is talking, or if you are constantly interrupting with your thoughts, you are lacking a crucial skill for successful marriage.

- **Are you a critic?** Critics don't make good marriage partners. If you are always finding faults in people and especially in your partner and then expressing the best fixes so everyone and everything meets your high standards, let me be your critic for a moment: You will be a bad marriage partner.

- **Are you clear with your meaning, or are you often misunderstood?** If you can't communicate clearly so your partner has a clue as to what you are talking about, this means you are missing a major marriage skill you will most certainly need to be a successful spouse.

- **Can you readily admit that you are wrong?** If you are a person who always needs to be right, you aren't going to be right for marriage. And if you are too insecure to humbly admit when you are wrong, you need to work on some stuff.

- **How are you at saying sorry?** "Sorry" is one of the most important words uttered in successful marriages. So, if you have a hard time saying it (and meaning it), you are, I'm sorry to say, lacking a significant marriage skill.

- **Are you good at seeing tasks and chores that need to be done and then taking care of them before being told about them?** If you are a lazy, entitled, inattentive, procrastinating person who expects everyone else to handle stuff for you, you lack many obvious skills necessary for a happy, successful marriage.

- **Do you pay attention to the things that are most important to others and make sure those 'important things' become important to you?** If your world and happiness are the only important things to you, you need to alter how you operate if you want a successful marriage.

- **Do you know how to make someone else feel special by giving favorite gifts and/or doing favorite deeds for someone without it being a birthday or anniversary?** (If you don't remember birthdays or anniversaries, you are immediately disqualified for marriage.) If you don't think about ways to bless your partner and/or don't carry out ways to make people feel special, you need to add this skill.

- **Ever had a roommate? What was that situation like? What would your past roommates say about you?** If you have been roommates with anyone (siblings included) and they would give you a one-star review, you probably need to find out what made you get such a bad review and work to correct your bad behaviors/attitudes.

- **How do you teach people a lesson if they do wrong?** If you hold grudges and punish people severely for making mistakes, you will not have a successful marriage (but you might make a good Russian dictator).

- **What do you get stubborn about?** If you dig in your heels about small stuff and refuse to budge or compromise on issues with people, you need some re-training in this area before you can expect a happy, successful marriage.

- **Are you easily stressed out, and do you make the people around you experience your stress?** If small stuff makes you all panicky and you drag others into your stress reactions all the time, you are probably not going to have a happy spouse (unless you marry a mannequin).

- **Are you manipulative?** If you are the sort of person who uses guilt, shame, tricks, and tactics to get your way all the time, you are a dangerous candidate for marriage. Mr. T pities the fool who marries you.

- **Are you a liar or consistently deceptive?** If you are not honest, even when it costs you, you are not qualified for marriage. You must learn the skill of honesty.

- **Are you good at interviews but bad at doing the actual work?** If you are a great interviewer but a lousy worker, you are only good for dating but probably not made for marriage. Successful marriages require constant work – don't get yourself hired by someone only to disappoint them.

- **Are you a needy person? Are you demanding? Are you high maintenance?**

You probably need to ask others to answer this one for you...or maybe you know you are. If you are a combo of needy, demanding, and high maintenance, you need a full-on skill set reset.

- **What are your insecurities, and do these insecurities dictate your actions and words with others?** If you are insecure and relate accordingly, you don't have the emotional skills necessary for a successful marriage.

- **Are you a know-it-all who loves to let others know that you know it all?** If so, you are annoying and will have a better chance on *Jeopardy* than in the marriage game.

- **How do you argue?** If you stab with cruel, personal knives when you argue, you are not marriage safe. You need to learn to skillfully discuss and disagree.

- **How much do you care about what others think?** If you have major perception worry and mainly do things based on how you think others will respond, you will most likely not have a happy marriage.

- **Are you a packrat or a hoarder?** If you own storage sheds filled with other people's garage sale junk or if you fill every possible space in your house with trinkets, knick-knacks, and stacks of old National Geographics, you need to learn the skill of simplicity (and trash-canning) before embarking on marriage.

- **Are you an OCD clean freak?** Being neat and tidy is great. But if you need your environment to be a medically clean space, you need to get some therapy before getting married. Relationships can be filthy.

- **Are you such a mama's boy or daddy's girl that you put one or both of your parents on hero pedestals?** Adults who refuse to stop leaning on mommy and/or daddy for advice, comfort, approval, money, etc., are not mature and thus must fit into the "disqualified for successful marriage" category. Marriage means leaving behind your parents as your caregivers and trading in their care for your chosen person's care. If you aren't willing to let go of your parents' control over you and swing entirely over to the trapeze bar of your spouse, you should not get married. (If this is your problem, you might have a co-dependency issue that requires serious counseling. A great therapist can skill you up here.)

- **Have you ever been verbally, emotionally, physically, or sexually abusive in a relationship?** Hurting people is wrong – didn't we learned this in kindergarten? You need to get some serious re-training and become dedicated to non-violence in your relationships before you get married.

- **Have you ever been verbally, emotionally, physically, or sexually abused by anyone?** If you have been hit in any of these areas (stats say about 80% of people have been), you need to get yourself some EMDR (Google it), some spiritual healing, and some trauma counseling. If you don't chase professional healing for these events and instead choose to walk around as a broken person with sharp shards sticking out of you, you will not have a successful marriage. Get thyself to a life mechanic ASAP.

- **Are you an addict who refuses to struggle against your addictions?** There are plenty of "fixers" and "enablers" out there for you in the dating pool, but please disqualify yourself from destroying a marriage partner. If your spouse isn't going to be your "drug of choice," avoid spousing.

****

So, that's the end of the quiz.

How did you do?

Are you the one-in-a-million super-skilled spouse who is set for marriage success?

Or are you more similar to me 25 years ago – a self-centered, lazy, and prideful know-it-all who lacked a bunch of the skills crucial for marital success?

Don't worry about it if, like me, you totally bombed that quiz and aren't anywhere close to being currently qualified for marriage. Being unskilled right now doesn't mean you can't become a skilled spouse. McDonald's workers might not start out as amazing employees who can master a register, make a killer McRib, properly change out urinal cakes, and keep the dining room free of fallen French fries. But

107

with the proper training, they get there. The same goes for you. It might be a good idea to get a good life coach, pastor, accountability partner, truth-telling friend, and excellent counselor to get you ready to become qualified for a successful marriage.

You might be a sucky candidate for marriage at this moment, but with the awareness (that hopefully came from these questions), some good introspection, some trained trainers, and a lot of help from the Holy Spirit, you too might become the best dang spouse on the planet. (Even if it takes years of in-the-marriage training for you to become "employee/spouse of the year," take heart, have hope, keep training, and know you will get there. I've been married for almost three decades, and I am still making slow progress and honing my spousal skills. I thank God for a patient wife!)

*A critical author's note: Sadly, most un-qualified people find someone who is googly-eyed and gush-hearted enough to say "I Do" to them before this training happens. I expect misery for them in the long run. I plead with you not to be a misery maker. Please take my questions seriously, admit your lack of skills, and start your journey toward becoming the best spouse you can be.

Reality #9: You don't know enough about the person you are falling for! But you could, and you should!

Reality #9: You don't know enough about the person you are falling for! But you could, and you should!

Diving into a lifetime relationship without gathering as much information about your future partner is foolishness. So let me continue to help you get to know your partner, so we cut down on post "I Do" surprises.

Here are some exercises you should try out to KNOW yourself and your significant other better before walking down that aisle:

The FUAQs

    A. Road Trip

    B. Dealbreakers

    C. Worldview

    D. Objectives

It's time to start FUAQing!

Too many Christians I know wait to **FUAQ** until they are married, and this is a mistake. I know this might seem a little controversial in a Christian book, but I suggest you start **FUAQing** each other as soon as possible. I think you should **FUAQ** with each other as much as you can.

FUAQing will help build your intimacy. FUAQing will make you both feel better. FUAQing will build your bond.

FUAQ now. FUAQ later.

FUAQ at home. FUAQ at church.

It's fun to FUAQ.

But before you start **FUAQing**, let me clarify what I mean when I use the **FUAQ** acronym. **FUAQ** stands for **F**requently **U**n**A**nswered

Questions, and **FUAQing** is the act of asking and answering the **Frequently UnAnswered Questions**, which are essential to a successful marriage.

So, have you started FUAQing?

If not, you need to. I am not expecting you to take all **my FUAQ exercises** on at one time. But if you and your partner will commit to asking and answering all the **FUAQs** below, you will be a long way down the road to understanding any problems you might face in your relationship.

Now without further ado, let's jump into the proverbial SACK and take on our first set of FUAQs.

A. The FUAQing Road Trip: I recommend taking a road trip with your partner and tackling the following questions, so you know each other as well as you can.

*If you could do anything with your life, what would you do?

*What are the biggest disappointments in your life thus far?

*What is your biggest loss?

*What are your top three biggest regrets?

*If you could go back and make a different decision about anything, what would you go back and do?

*Perceive yourself: Physically; Potential; Abilities; Style; Intelligence; etc.

*What are three specific behaviors you want to improve?

*How do you view money? Are you in debt? Do you have great/good/decent/horrific credit?

*Any felonies or misdemeanors I don't know about?

*What would be your perfect vacation?

*What is your political platform?

*What embarrasses you?

*How much time do you spend on social media? Watching TV? Playing video games?

*What are you addicted to? Gambling? Pornography? Social Media? TV? Food? Caffeine?

115

*What are you insecure about?

*What in the world are you most passionate about?

*What are your expectations for life?

*What equals a successful day for you?

*How much do you care about what other people think about you?

*How would your best friends describe you?

*Do you have enemies?

*What did you want to be when you were a kid?

*Besides hanging out with me, what equals fun to you?

*What equals a fun date night for you?

*How much time do you like to spend alone?

*What is your personality type? (Check out the book *Type Talk* or take a Myers-Briggs Assessment for a more complete understanding of personality.)

*If I could help you achieve any dream for your life, what would that dream be, and how do you see me playing a part?

*What types of compliments or affirmations mean something to you?

*What kinds of words hurt you the most?

*Do you make a big deal out of certain holidays?

*When you come home from your workday, what is your ideal 'unwind'?

*What is your motivation for getting married? What is driving you to get married?

*How much do you tip, no matter the level of service?

*How do you act/react when things don't go your way?

*How do you define clean?

*How important is personal hygiene to you?

*Bathroom door open or shut during poop sessions?

*How important is modesty?

*How important is staying fit and healthy to you?

*What is the best way to handle a disagreement?

*What are you like when you are sick? How do you like to be treated/cared for when sick?

*How do you try to get your way?

*Are you judgmental about anything?

*What is your current bucket list?

*What are your favorite things? Snacks? Drinks? Surprises? Foods? Restaurants? Movies? Bands? Styles? Books?

*What is your decision-making process? How do you make decisions?

*Do you like to be surprised? Celebrated?

*What annoys you the most about how people act? What annoys you about me?

*What roles did you have as a kid? Do you still play those roles? Do you want to retire from any of those roles?

*How did your parents show you love?

*Have you ever been rejected, and how did that affect you? Ever experienced abandonment? How did that impact you?

*Do you have any life traumas that haven't been dealt with?

*Are you easily offended? What offends you? What words or actions trigger you or cause you to knee-jerk with a negative reaction?

*How do you deal with people being sad or depressed around you?

*How do you deal with stress?

*What life/home chores do you prefer, and which ones do you despise?

*Do you flirt with people of the opposite sex? What equals crossing the line? How do you define flirting?

*If you could change anything about your current life situation, what would you change?

*Ever experienced sexual or physical abuse? How did that impact you?

*How do you comfort yourself? Make yourself feel better when circumstances are tough?

*Are you an aggressive investor or a safety-first one?

*What are your spiritual goals? How will you achieve them?

*How do you see God? How do you think He sees you?

*What is your favorite book of the Bible? What are your favorite verses?

*What is the best life advice you've ever received?

*What family traditions do you want to carry forward into marriage?

*How are you at confrontation?

*How much do you think culture influences you?

*What people in the media and entertainment do you listen to about life and why?

*Have you ever been sure you were making the right moves and decisions but ended up in a bad spot? How did you react? What did you learn from this?

*How much do you trust me? Trust yourself?

*How important is having sex to you?

*What sexual desires or fantasies would you like fulfilled in our marriage?

*How do you feel about getting counseling or life coaching?

*What do you want people to say about you when you are dead?

*What are your thoughts about drinking socially? Getting drunk?

*Tell me about your past romantic relationships. What ended them? What did you learn from them? In what ways do you think our relationship is different from those past relationships?

How much do you think is appropriate to spend on the wedding ceremony and reception?

*What are the essentials for a wedding ceremony?

*Have you ever been fooled or deceived?

*Are you quick to listen, slow to speak, and slow to become angry?

*What things make you angry?

*How do you treat people you are angry with?

*How do you deal with feeling attracted to others? Do you see attraction as normal? When does it cross a line?

*Are you quick to forgive and offer grace to those who let you down?

*What are things that would mean an immediate end to our relationship?

*What hurts your feelings?

*What would you **deem "harmless habits"** that should be allowed?

*Why do you think I like you?

*Do you have a preferred side of the bed, or is this negotiable?

*What things would you put on your relational **résumé**?

*What things would you put on your anti-résumé? In other words, what idiosyncrasies, weirdnesses, gross habits, unattractive actions, etc., do you have that you would never include on your relational résumé? What strange things don't I know about you yet? (Examples: "I pick my nose and eat what I pull out." Or "I like to sing *John Jacob Jingleheimer Schmidt* one hundred times a day.")

*How will we know if we are making good progress towards intimacy in our marriage?

*What life dream of yours would be the hardest to let go of?

*What do you want to learn about? What skills do you want to gain?

*What skills can I learn that will be most beneficial to you? Make life better for you or help your dreams come true?

*What do you think is your reputation?

*What are your fears?

*What do you think our marriage will be like in 5 years? 10 years? 20 years? 30 years?

*What about your parents' marriage do you most admire? Want to avoid?

*What do I do now that you hope I never stop doing? What do I do that you hope I outgrow?

*What generational problems or family tendencies do you hope to break?

*Our marriage will be a successful, happy one if...

*The most common reasons why people divorce are as follows: "We just grew apart," "I fell out of love with them," "No romance/The spark was gone," "I found someone else who suits me better," "My spouse changed," "Financial problems," "Got married too young/before I was ready," "My spouse is selfish," "My spouse just doesn't get me," Adultery, Addiction, etc.)

*Why do *you* think 3 out of 5 marriages between couples (somewhat similar to us) end in divorce?

*Knowing the statistics and the commonly claimed reasons listed above, what can we do to make sure we last?

B. FUAQing Potential Dealbreakers

In this section, I ask you to score or scale various things to help you discover what is important to you and your spouse.

For each thing listed below, give it a score based on the explanations below.

1-3 – "No way I'm doing/having that in my marriage. I do not want and will not have this in my marriage world."

4-5 – "This doesn't matter too much to me; I defer to my spouse's wishes."

6-7 – "I'm open to compromise on this one. But what I think about it is fairly important."

8-10 – "I absolutely must have this in my marriage world. This is an expectation I can't let go of."

Recommendation: Score each of these without your partner around, adding your specifics to those requiring it. For instance, "I am a total 10 on being a united Republican/**Democratic** Party household." Or "I am a 1 on pets. I don't ever want any pet in my marriage world." Or "I am a 9 on having my own kids and an 8 on having 7 of them, but I am a 6 regarding their names."

Be honest on your scoring and specifics – do not score based on what you think your partner will want you to say. This is a huge deal, and you will regret it later if you scored these just trying to be "hopefully" agreeable. This scoring will reveal what is super important or unimportant to you about matters that can determine the future success of your marriage.

Lie about these now and pay for it later.

Having kids at all

My Answer:

1_____5_____10

"No Way"   "Defer"   "Must Have"

My Partner's Answer:

1_____5_____10

"No Way"   "Defer"   "Must Have"

Why did you answer the way you did?

Explanations/Arguments and Notes:

Having kids of our own

My Answer:

1_____5_____10

"No Way"   "Defer"   "Must Have"

My Partner's Answer:

1_____5_____10

"No Way"   "Defer"   "Must Have"

Why did you answer the way you did?

Explanations/Arguments and Notes:

Having a specific number of kids

My Answer:

1_____5_____10

"No Way"   "Defer"   "Must Have"

My Partner's Answer:

1_____5_____10

"No Way"   "Defer"   "Must Have"

Why did you answer the way you did?

Explanations/Arguments and Notes:

Having specific names for kids

My Answer:

1_____5_____10

"No Way"   "Defer"   "Must Have"

My Partner's Answer:

1_____5_____10

"No Way"   "Defer"   "Must Have"

Why did you answer the way you did?

Explanations/Arguments and Notes:

Certain styles of discipline
for our kids

My Answer:

1_____5_____10

"No Way"   "Defer"   "Must Have"

My Partner's Answer:

1_____5_____10

"No Way"   "Defer"   "Must Have"

Why did you answer the way you did?

Explanations/Arguments and Notes:

Homeschooling, private schooling, public schooling?

My Answer:

1_____5_____10

"No Way"   "Defer"   "Must Have"

My Partner's Answer:

1_____5_____10

"No Way"   "Defer"   "Must Have"

Why did you answer the way you did?

Explanations/Arguments and Notes:

Having specific pets
with specific names

My Answer:

1_____5_____10

"No Way"   "Defer"   "Must Have"

My Partner's Answer:

1_____5_____10

"No Way"   "Defer"   "Must Have"

Why did you answer the way you did?

Explanations/Arguments and Notes:

Pets live inside or outside

My Answer:

1_____5_____10

"No Way"   "Defer"   "Must Have"

My Partner's Answer:

1_____5_____10

"No Way"   "Defer"   "Must Have"

Why did you answer the way you did?

Explanations/Arguments and Notes:

Living in a certain size house
in a particular type of neighborhood

My Answer:

1_____5_____10

"No Way"   "Defer"   "Must Have"

My Partner's Answer:

1_____5_____10

"No Way"   "Defer"   "Must Have"

Why did you answer the way you did?

Explanations/Arguments and Notes:

A certain Standard of Living expectation

My Answer:

1_____5_____10

"No Way"   "Defer"   "Must Have"

My Partner's Answer:

1_____5_____10

"No Way"   "Defer"   "Must Have"

Why did you answer the way you did?

Explanations/Arguments and Notes:

Specific car? Leasing or buying?

My Answer:

1_____5_____10

"No Way"   "Defer"   "Must Have"

My Partner's Answer:

1_____5_____10

"No Way"   "Defer"   "Must Have"

Why did you answer the way you did?

Explanations/Arguments and Notes:

Debt spending or always debt-free?

My Answer:

1_____5_____10

"No Way"   "Defer"   "Must Have"

My Partner's Answer:

1_____5_____10

"No Way"   "Defer"   "Must Have"

Why did you answer the way you did?

Explanations/Arguments and Notes:

Buying what you want when you want

My Answer:

1_____5_____10

"No Way"   "Defer"   "Must Have"

My Partner's Answer:

1_____5_____10

"No Way"   "Defer"   "Must Have"

Why did you answer the way you did?

Explanations/Arguments and Notes:

Political leanings a certain way?
Specific parties or platforms?

My Answer:

1_____5_____10

"No Way"   "Defer"   "Must Have"

My Partner's Answer:

1_____5_____10

"No Way"   "Defer"   "Must Have"

Why did you answer the way you did?

Explanations/Arguments and Notes:

Weekly Church attendance

My Answer:

1_____5_____10

"No Way"   "Defer"   "Must Have"

My Partner's Answer:

1_____5_____10

"No Way"   "Defer"   "Must Have"

Why did you answer the way you did?

Explanations/Arguments and Notes:

Yearly vacations to specific locations

My Answer:

1_____5_____10

"No Way"   "Defer"   "Must Have"

My Partner's Answer:

1_____5_____10

"No Way"   "Defer"   "Must Have"

Why did you answer the way you did?

Explanations/Arguments and Notes:

Weekly time spent with others/friends

My Answer:

1_____5_____10

"No Way"   "Defer"   "Must Have"

My Partner's Answer:

1_____5_____10

"No Way"   "Defer"   "Must Have"

Why did you answer the way you did?

Explanations/Arguments and Notes:

Living in the same city as my family

My Answer:

1_____5_____10

"No Way"   "Defer"   "Must Have"

My Partner's Answer:

1_____5_____10

"No Way"   "Defer"   "Must Have"

Why did you answer the way you did?

Explanations/Arguments and Notes:

Specific interior design of living space

My Answer:

1_____5_____10

"No Way"   "Defer"   "Must Have"

My Partner's Answer:

1_____5_____10

"No Way"   "Defer"   "Must Have"

Why did you answer the way you did?

Explanations/Arguments and Notes:

Having or maintaining close relationships with the opposite sex

My Answer:

1_____5_____10

"No Way"   "Defer"   "Must Have"

My Partner's Answer:

1_____5_____10

"No Way"   "Defer"   "Must Have"

Why did you answer the way you did?

Explanations/Arguments and Notes:

Frequent passionate sex

My Answer:

1_____5_____10

"No Way"   "Defer"   "Must Have"

My Partner's Answer:

1_____5_____10

"No Way"   "Defer"   "Must Have"

Why did you answer the way you did?

Explanations/Arguments and Notes:

Daily family dinner at the table

My Answer:

1_____5_____10

"No Way"　　　　"Defer"　　　　"Must Have"

My Partner's Answer:

1_____5_____10

"No Way"　　　　"Defer"　　　　"Must Have"

Why did you answer the way you did?

Explanations/Arguments and Notes:

Control of the remote control

My Answer:

1_____5_____10

"No Way"   "Defer"   "Must Have"

My Partner's Answer:

1_____5_____10

"No Way"   "Defer"   "Must Have"

Why did you answer the way you did?

Explanations/Arguments and Notes:

Full-on holiday decorations

My Answer:

1_____5_____10

"No Way"   "Defer"   "Must Have"

My Partner's Answer:

1_____5_____10

"No Way"   "Defer"   "Must Have"

Why did you answer the way you did?

Explanations/Arguments and Notes:

*Once you have done this individual scoring and added your specifics, it's time to come together and discuss your scores. Hopefully, you don't have any 1's versus 10's because that means you have what I call a **pre-marriage dealbreaker** on your hands. For instance, if you absolutely do not want kids and your partner says he/she absolutely must, this is a massive problem that needs to be brought to a trained counselor. Or if you are a 2 on having more than one kid and they are a 9 on having three or more kids, this too represents a major problem in need of a mediator who can help you determine if this relationship needs to go any further.

I have had experience with one pre-marriage couple who had several dealbreakers they refused to acknowledge as serious problems. One of their issues that had the greatest variance or gap was living in the same city as one of their parents. The female said she was a 9-10 on living in the same city as her parents, while the male said his job opportunities were too limited by this. He already had a job he loved in a city located nine hours away and wasn't willing to quit it so his future spouse could live in the same city as her parents.

A major problem, right?

Well, even though neither of them was willing to compromise on their demands/desires/expectations, they didn't see a need to postpone or cancel their wedding over this. They ignored the counsel and got married anyway. They both gambled on this very common but dumb assumption: "I can change my spouse's mind."

Where is this couple now?

What happened with this couple?

The woman "lovingly" pressured her husband until the man quit his job with a ton of resentment and moved with his wife to the city where her parents lived. The man found a decent job there but was super angry that his wife put her strong desires over his strong desires.

They are divorced now.

Lesson to learn: Don't ignore my counsel? No. Lots of people ignore me and survive just fine.

The real lessons here:

- **Take seriously wide gaps/wide variance on issues.**

- **Don't blow off what is super important to your partner.**

157

- **Don't think "changing their mind" will lead you anywhere good.**

Please pay special attention to the areas where there is a wide variance between you and your partner. Where significant gaps exist, major relational problems originate. Big gaps force big compromises and big issues, leading to anger, resentment, bitterness, and especially disappointment.

*One must realize that keeping anger, resentment, bitterness, and disappointment at minimum levels is crucial for marital health.

So, if you did discover big gaps between you and your partner when you scaled the above, do not ignore them or wish them away. Find a counselor who can help you determine the best ways to bridge these gaps before it is too late.

C. FUAQing Worldviews: It is important to have a conversation about how your partner sees the world so you can have some sort of idea as to how they are going to deal with life. **Knowing how they see the world and life in a macro way will help you know what to expect from them and give you the blueprints you can call them back to if you ever see them stray from what they have decided is the best way to see/perceive.**

I will give an example worldview, which happens to be mine, so you can have a launching off point.

Ben's Worldview

--I am just a speck. One of seven billion on a tiny planet in a tiny galaxy within a vast universe following the lead of generations of billions who have set up a gameboard for us but who are now dead.

--As a speck, I do mostly smaller speck-level things. Speck-level things are mostly minuscule. There are no BIG things, even if other specks tell me there are. So while I must do speck-level things every day of my life, I won't super-size any of them despite others' claims that a lot is riding on a specific speck-task. This removes any personal pressure or stress. I can act freely, do my best to create positive outcomes, and never worry about how those outcomes land.

--There is no big game, big meeting, big test, big _____. How we elevate the consequences tied to the event or task will determine if we see anything as big or small. Fear of "our" worst-case scenarios, which is usually tied to insecurities that are often linked to real traumas, drives this elevation! "Who cares?" and "So what?" are key phrases to use a lot in our thoughts that drive our emotions and actions.

--My proper speck-level sizing is based on this: Everything I do that is not for God's glory or under His command is meaningless. While it may have an effect, it holds no real importance. Most of life is a silly game. Speck-stuff is just chasing after the wind.

--Many specks around me don't think as I do, and thus, they try to be the biggest speck-fish in the biggest speck-ponds, chasing after game objectives I could not care less about. They might even try manipulative tactics and form various sketchy alliances to gain control of larger sections of this planetary gameboard. I won't judge them, but I won't be fooled into elevating the small things or small people to places of significance like they do.

--Speck-media, speck-politicians, and speck-marketers exist to super-spin and super-size issues and products, so I will care about them enough that I will give them my attention and my money. I appreciate their trying to distract me from the boredom of this life, but I will mostly ignore their pleas.

--Speck-products can be entertaining, useful, convenient, and/or exciting. But they are really not worth much in the long run. So I will own some speck-products but will always be willing to leave them behind at the drop of a hat. I'll not hold too tightly to that which I cannot take with me beyond this planet.

--Knowing that other people outside of media and marketing are also specks, I don't have to care too much about what they think about me. People's perceptions are flawed because their experiences and knowledge are limited. I will not give myself over to them whether they think me worthy of kingship or martyrdom. My identity as God's loved speck is set, and no other speck can add to that or subtract from it.

--Governments, corporations, schools, Think Tanks, and every other organization is just a group of specks. Just because they have formed some sort of 'powerful' union and have re-branded accordingly does not mean they are anything more than groups of 'grown-up babies' trying to influence other speck behavior. Just because a "big" company, "expert" agency, or "reputed" university spreads information or makes rules does not mean I need to believe them or bow down to them. I will not make decisions based on "grouped" speck thoughts and/or policies. I pray, seek God, and move according to His 'policies.'

--All specks are created by and loved by God and thus must be loved by me. Seeing myself as but a speck makes it easier to be humble and even to lay down my speck-life for those around me.

--My speck-death is imminent. During the time I do have, I want to be a humble and grateful speck who uses what God has given me to impact the lives of the neediest specks within my sphere of influence, especially with regard to their eternal future.

--As a speck, I will not be remembered for very long after my death. Making speck history is not my goal. I'm not here to have buildings named after me. I don't even want or need a quality obituary or eulogy. As long as the speck-Maker remembers me on the other side, I am good to go. This saves me from trying to do what is "memorable" and frees me up to do what is kind and just.

(Most specks, even the most ripple-causing, intelligent, and famous specks, are forgotten long before their deaths. Specks tend to 'radar-blip,' then fade.)

--I have a lot in common with the specks around me (loss, pain, troubles, options, preferences, families, traumas, stresses, barriers, temptations, desires, etc.), but what they are after, I am not. Still, it is good to think of my other specks as **more similar** to than completely different from me. Our shared realities help form the basis of my re'speck't for others.

--Life is a game lived on a gameboard. Every day I have a new turn, but my rules and objectives are different from my fellow game players' rules and objectives. As a result, my success is defined differently than almost everyone else's.

--Most specks I know chase after the following "game" objectives: Pleasure, Power, Influence, Fame, Wealth, Love, Happiness, Health, Purpose/Meaning, Strength, Beauty, Style, Spirituality, Intelligence, and/or Possessions, and I will be tempted to go after them, too. But since the methods used to achieve them are typically joyless and busy grabs for what falls short of any version of lasting satisfaction (*The Matrix* Blue Pill), I pray I quickly notice any shifts of MO and exit ramp back onto my narrow, alien path toward more profound satisfaction.

--No other speck can ruin my life. They might ruin moments or seasons, but I have the choice to respond with resilience and grace.

--Some specks may try to hurt me, control me, and/or use me for their base ends, but I choose whether or not to let them.

--My speck-life is guided by the Bible, and thus, I need to know what the point of the Bible is: to introduce me to God, Jesus, and the Holy Spirit and to show me how to gain and maintain intimacy with them. As well, it tells me what I can be certain of no matter what is happening in my world. Faith is certainty. I must ask daily what I am certain of and why I am uncertain of other ideas. Do I have a 'no matter what' kind of faith or an 'if this, then' type of faith?

(My "certainty" will be tested, so I will probably find out.)

***That's my worldview.

*What do you think about that per'speck'tive?

*Which things do you agree with? Which points do you have a hard time with?

Now let's turn this over to you.

It's time to consider this: What is *my* firmly established perspective on life and the world, and how does it serve me? Also, how might this perspective serve my spouse?

Once both of you have written out a basic perspective, then compare, contrast, and discuss how each of your worldviews might serve you as a couple.

My Worldview

*

*

*

*

*

*

*

*

*

My Partner's Worldview

*

*

*

*

*

*

*

*

*

D. FUAQing Objectives: Most people don't set out clear life objectives for themselves, or at least, most people don't know what objectives they actually serve. But it is key to have a set of general objectives you are aware of and acting on so you know if you are actually accomplishing what you woke up each day trying to accomplish.

It is probably a good idea to have each person in the relationship create his or her own objectives list and then have the couple create a set of shared objectives, which define "winning."

Again, I have included my own objectives as a starting point for you as you write out your own. Your objectives can be totally different than mine. That's totally fine. My objectives define daily success for me, and your objectives should define your daily success.

174

Ben's Objectives

I have five main objectives that determine daily actions on life's gameboard, **and I prioritize them like this:**

-Seek God's face earnestly and beyond theology.

-**Pray with power to demolish all cultural and enemy arguments set up against the knowledge of God.**

-**Love the ones in front of you as you are led and empowered by the Spirit.**

-**Make disciples who are wide awake but not "woke."**

-Do 'just' things in a world dominated by injustice, starting with 'kids in crisis' as your number one target population

Those are my daily objectives. Now you and your partner can create your own and then try to discover shared objectives.

Remember, the goal of setting your objectives is to decide what actions you will focus on every day so that at the end of each day, you can determine if you accomplished what you have decided equals success.

My Objectives

*

*

*

*

*

*

*

*

My Partner's Objectives

*

*

*

*

*

*

*

*

Okay, okay, enough FUAQing for now.

You've probably been FUAQing for hours and hours and feel super tired. Grab a nap if you must.

I recall my first few times FUAQing my fiancée, and it totally wore me out. But it felt really good to do it, and it made a significant difference in our relationship. Pre-marital FUAQing helped us get to know each other better and showed us some areas we needed to talk about with a professional.

I hope this initial FUAQing with your partner did the same for you. Like my wife and me, I also hope that you both will become lifelong FUAQers, who keep asking and answering new questions that pop up in life.

Being interested and staying interested in your partner is essential. Lifelong FUAQing keeps the communication channels open and deepens intimacy in marriages.

Author's note: If you did these FUAQing exercises, you probably know more about your partner than 90% of the couples out there. I think this is a good thing for you and a terrible thing for them. Some would argue and say, "Ignorance is Bliss," but I would bet that your informed marriage will be much better than their ignorant ones.

The End of the Book

The End of the Book:

Well, congratulations! You made it to the end of the book, and hopefully, you learned a whole lot about yourself and your partner that you can use to head toward marriage as informed lovers who are ready to say "I Do" to a forever love.

As I have said before, I recommend that you take this now well-worn book with you to a professional therapist or pastoral, pre-marital superstar and ask them to help you learn how to best use the knowledge you have gained.

With that, I bid thee adieu and invite you to check out book two in this series: *The Ultimate Marriage Survival Guide* after you have returned from your honeymoon fun or after you hit some trouble. I wish you the best possible relationship with God as your third and most important partner. May He bless you

182

in your ever-growing intimacy with Him and with one another!

ABOUT THE AUTHOR:

Seasoned Life Coach, Ordained Spiritual Director, Genre-bending Author, Relationship Guide, and self-proclaimed Deep Thinker, Ben Donley permanently exists in Lubbock, Texas, after living everywhere from Guangzhou, China, to Los Angeles, California.

Ben, a Bible-believing Christian, credits God for helping him overcome severe depression and anxiety.

His priorities are intimacy with the Lord, love for others, and compassionate justice (especially for sexually trafficked children).

What I Wish I Knew Before I Said "I Do" is his 14th book.

If you liked this book, give it a five-star rating, and check out some of his others:

*The Things I Think I Think
*Down In It
*The New Christian Whatever

Unplugged: A Matrix Bible Study
I Guess "I Do:" The Ultimate Marriage Survival Guide
MeZuss
The Tiny Bang

If you would like to send Ben a message, book him as a speaker, or personally harangue him, reach out through the general contact page at dreamloudpublishing.com. You can also engage with him through his website for this book at **www.FUAQing.com.**

186

Made in the USA
Columbia, SC
17 September 2022

67376713R00102